Handel

HANDEL

by
STANLEY SADIE

THOMAS Y. CROWELL COMPANY

New York

First published in the United States of America in 1969

Copyright © 1968 by Stanley Sadie

Printed in Great Britain

Library of Congress Catalog Card No. 68-29474

Contents

Illustrations

Illustrations

Grateful acknowledgements are made to *The Musical Times* for permission to use the material for Figures 1, 19 and 21; to the Handel House, Halle, for Plate I and Figures 2, 3 and 6; to the Trustees of the British Museum for Plates III–XII and Figures 4, 5, 7, 9, 11, 13, 14, 16, 18 and 20; and to the National Portrait Gallery for Plate XIII.

Music Examples

(all by Handel)

Handel

I

Boyhood in Germany

The pattern of musical history sometimes seems rather like a mountain range: a few large peaks, a lot of medium-sized and small ones. And as with mountains, the larger ones tend to come in groups. Haydn and Mozart wrote their greatest music at about the same time; so did Beethoven and Schubert; so did Wagner and Brahms.

Handel and Bach were even more exact contemporaries than any of these pairs. They were born in 1685, within four weeks of one another, and less than a hundred miles apart; Domenico Scarlatti was born the same year, and Rameau and Telemann were still in infancy. The period of musical history which we call the Baroque was brought to a glorious close by these men, and by Bach and Handel in particular.

Although we are inclined to regard Handel as an Englishman—after all, he wrote the greatest single work in the English language—he was German born and Italian trained. His birthplace was the Saxon town of Halle, not

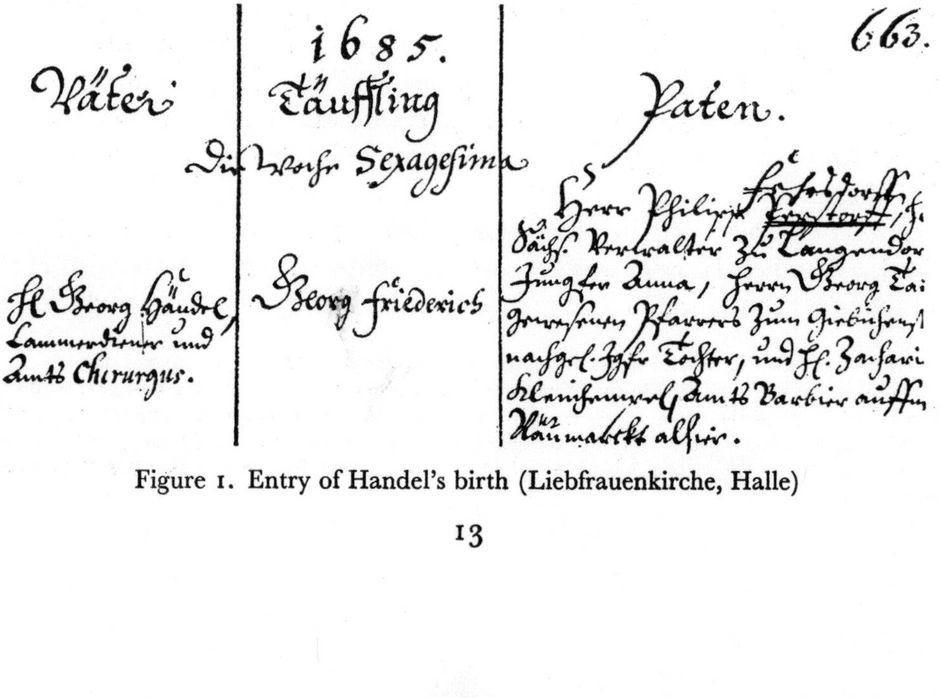

Figure 1. Entry of Handel's birth (Liebfrauenkirche, Halle)

far from Leipzig. Unlike Bach and Scarlatti, who were both born into families with long and strong musical traditions, Handel was brought up in a home where little music was heard. His father was a medical man, a barber-surgeon, and at the time of George Frideric's[1] birth he was in his sixties, a much respected figure in Halle.

We don't know much about the early years of Handel's life. Nobody in those days, of course, chronicled the life of the barber-surgeon's small son—they couldn't have guessed that he would turn out to be a musical genius—and although Handel himself, some sixty or seventy years later, told his first biographer (an English clergyman) something about his life, his recollection by then was somewhat hazy.

What we do know is that his father didn't much care for music as a career for his only son. Possibly he didn't like music at all; Handel's gifts may have been inherited mainly on his mother's side. As a boy, he must have come into contact with music at church and probably at school. It wasn't encouraged at home, except perhaps by his aunt Anna, his mother's sister: there is a story of the boy smuggling a clavichord (a small, very quiet keyboard instrument) into the house and practising in an attic when his parents were sound asleep.

So although the young Handel showed definite signs of strong musical gifts his father firmly guided him towards a career in law—a safe, respectable profession, certainly safer and more respectable than music. But on the insistence of a local nobleman, who had been mightily impressed on hearing the young boy play the organ, he allowed him to study music under the local church organist, Zachau, who was also a gifted composer. He was only about nine when he started these studies. They gave him a solid grounding in the technique of composition which later was to prove invaluable to him. He wrote a lot of church music during his studies, and music for the oboe: his earliest pieces to survive are a set of six sonatas for two oboes and continuo.[2] And not long after this time he wrote his oboe concertos, from which this minuet comes.

Handel's father died in 1697. The plans for a career in law still went ahead, and when Handel was seventeen he entered the University of Halle. But his heart remained in music, in which he was by now extremely skilled,

---

[1] We use the spelling of Handel's names which he adopted on taking British nationality.

[2] 'Continuo' is the term used in the seventeenth and eighteenth centuries for a bass part with small figures written above the notes: it was usually intended to be played on a sustaining instrument (like the cello) and a keyboard one (like the harpsichord or organ), with the keyboard player filling in with his right hand some supporting harmony—the figures indicated, in a sort of shorthand, the chords he was to play.

Oboe Concerto in B flat—finale

both as composer and performer. So when, in the same year, there was a vacancy at Halle Cathedral for a chief organist, he was appointed. The duties were not heavy; the cathedral was Calvinist (rather like Presbyterian) and not much music was used in the services. (Handel himself was a Lutheran; the Lutherans were, in their religious observance and their music, rather more like the Church of England.)

But Handel did not stay long in his new job. In 1703 he decided to leave home, to make his way in a wider musical world than Halle could offer. He set out for Hamburg: the obvious place to go, for it was a large, prosperous city—a 'free city', not under the dominion of some minor princeling, like most German centres—and it had a public opera house.

Figure 2. The Liebfrauenkirche in the market-place at Halle; Handel attended
this church and studied under its organist, Zachau

Handel's father

The house in Halle where Handel was born

Rome, Piazza Navona, showing the palace of Cardinal Panfili, where Handel performed

In Hamburg, Handel made a living by taking pupils and by playing second violin (and, later on, the harpsichord) in the opera-house orchestra. These must have been exciting times for him. He heard a bigger variety of

Figure 3. The Dom (cathedral) in Halle, where Handel was organist for a short time

music, met a bigger variety of people, than was possible in Halle—among them the opera-house director, Reinhard Keiser, and a young composer, Johann Mattheson. Handel and Mattheson became firm friends. They went together to Lübeck to compete for the post of organist there in succession to the famous Buxtehude, but it seems that one of the conditions of the job —marriage to Buxtehude's unattractive daughter—put them off. They exchanged lessons, Handel teaching Mattheson counterpoint, Mattheson teaching Handel the dramatic style. The young Handel evidently had a dry sense of humour: 'he behaved as though he didn't know how many beans made five', wrote Mattheson, years later. The two men once quarrelled, and even fought a duel, in which Handel might have been seriously hurt if Mattheson's sword had not struck a large button on his coat; but they settled the matter and remained firm friends for the rest of their lives.

It must have been an ambition fulfilled for Handel when early in 1705 his first opera, *Almira*, was performed in Hamburg. It was in a mixture of Italian and German—German for the parts where the story was told, so that the audience could understand, and Italian (the best language for singers) for some of the songs. *Almira* went down well with the Hamburg opera-goers,

B 17

but his second opera, *Nero*, was less successful when performed a few weeks later.

Handel wrote some other operas for Hamburg, but never heard them performed. They were given in 1708. By this time he was hundreds of miles away. Neither Hamburg nor any other German city was the right place for a young composer keen to make his mark in the world of opera. The only place was Italy. So, sometime in 1706, Handel once again packed his bags. Somehow he obtained the money needed for the long and expensive journey to Italy; possibly a wealthy patron paid for him. The next record of his presence anywhere comes from a diarist in Rome, who noted, in January 1707: 'A German has arrived here, an excellent harpsichordist and composer. Today he demonstrated his skill by playing the organ in the church of St. John, to the admiration of all who heard him.'

Figure 4. An early eighteenth-century view of Hamburg

II

'Il caro Sassone'

Italy, in Handel's time, was the cradle of opera, of oratorio and of the concerto. It was the land which every young composer wanted to visit. Handel went there as an inexperienced twenty-two-year-old, ready to learn; he came away, three years later, recognized as one of the most richly gifted composers of his day.

We don't know exactly what he did in Italy, or even where he spent much of his time. It is likely that for most of 1707 he was in Rome, which wasn't an opera centre: opera was banned at this time in the holy city. But instrumental music and oratorio flourished there. Handel met many of the rich Roman patrons of music, like Cardinal Ottoboni, and also met many of Italy's most famous composers: among them were the violinist Arcangelo Corelli (often regarded as the father of the trio sonata and concerto grosso), Alessandro Scarlatti (the leading opera composer of the time) and his young son Domenico—there is a story of a musical contest between Handel and Domenico Scarlatti, with Scarlatti the victor on the harpsichord and Handel on the organ.

After Rome, Handel went to Venice for a short time, meeting a prince from Hanover and the English ambassador there, and possibly meeting the composer Antonio Vivaldi, who was in charge of music at a Venetian girls' orphanage. Then back to Rome—where he had two oratorios performed, one at Easter 1708 and the other shortly after, both with Corelli leading the orchestra. Next on to Naples, where he wrote a 'serenata' to enliven the wedding festivities of a Neapolitan duke. Probably he visited Florence at some time (he may have had an opera produced there). By the end of 1709 he was back in Venice where, in December, his opera *Agrippina* was given.

This was a major triumph for Handel. The opera was greeted with cries of 'Viva il caro Sassone' ('Long live the beloved Saxon!') and had twenty-seven performances. By this time Handel had acquired a sure mastery of the graceful, flowing melodic style used by the Italians, as this music from the opera shows:

Agrippina: 'Se vuoi pace'

It was long practice, as well as his gifts, which gave Handel so sure a grasp of the Italian style. During his three years in Italy he composed about a hundred cantatas (short, ten-minute works for voice and continuo, sometimes with a violin or other instrument as well; usually they consisted of two songs, each preceded by a recitative). He also wrote some church music—for the Catholic Church, of course, in Italy, though he himself remained a staunch Protestant.

Agrippina's success made a splendid ending to Handel's years in Italy. Now twenty-five, he began to think about a permanent post; probably he had received some invitations, possibly actual offers, from the various noblemen he had met who employed musicians. Among the friends he had made in Italy may have been the composer Steffani, who had influence at the court of the Elector of Hanover. And he had met the Elector's brother. So it was there that Handel went from Italy, and in 1710 the Elector appointed him Kapellmeister (literally 'chapel-master'; in fact, director of music).

He was not there for long. Perhaps working at a small German court didn't seem very exciting after his Italian travels—no operas to write in Hanover, just chamber music to please the Elector and his family. So it's not

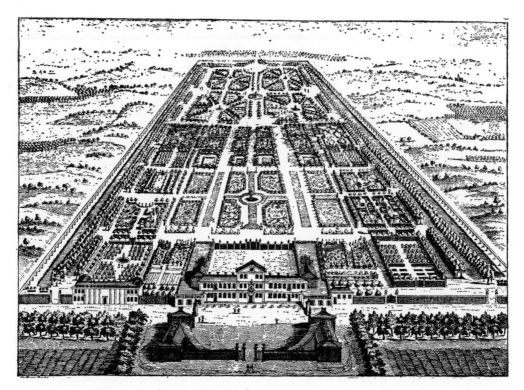

Figure 5. George I's estate at Herrenhausen, near Hanover

surprising that soon, after a mere four or five months, he asked for leave of absence. And it's not surprising, either, that with all Europe to choose from, he went to London. London was the richest city in the world, and musically one of the most active. Opera, and Italian music generally, were coming into fashion there. He had met several Englishmen in Italy, who no doubt had treated him with the courtesy for which English gentlemen were famed, and had suggested that he might care to visit their country.

So in autumn 1710 he set out from Hanover. Possibly he went through Halle, to see his mother. He called at Düsseldorf, playing before the Elector, who had invited him; and then, through Holland, on to England.

During this first visit to London Handel met many of the city's musical people. London was well known for its democratic musical life. There were musical societies which even fairly humble people could attend (in those days the gap between rich and poor was enormous); most famous was the weekly music meeting organized by a Clerkenwell coal-merchant, Thomas Britton—men and women from all ranks of society climbed the steep, cramped staircase to hear some of London's finest musicians play. Handel

Figure 6. From the manuscript of Handel's Brockes Passion

must have been puzzled by all this—there was nothing like it anywhere else —but he was surely happy to join in the music-making.

Handel quickly made the acquaintance of the man who organized London's operatic life, J. J. Heidegger. Heidegger introduced him to many influential and musical people. Handel played to one such person, whose ten-year-old niece was present; this little girl, who years later was to be a staunch friend to Handel, left an account of the occasion:

'We had no better instrument in the house than a little spinet of mine, on which the great musician performed wonders. I was much struck with his playing, but struck as a child, not a judge, for the moment he was gone, I seated myself at my instrument and played the best lessons I had then learnt. My uncle archly asked me if I thought I should ever play as well as Mr. Handel. "If I did not think I should," cried I, "I would burn my instrument!"'

Soon an opportunity came for an opera to be given. Handel worked fast, for the opera, *Rinaldo*, was to be staged in February; to speed up work he

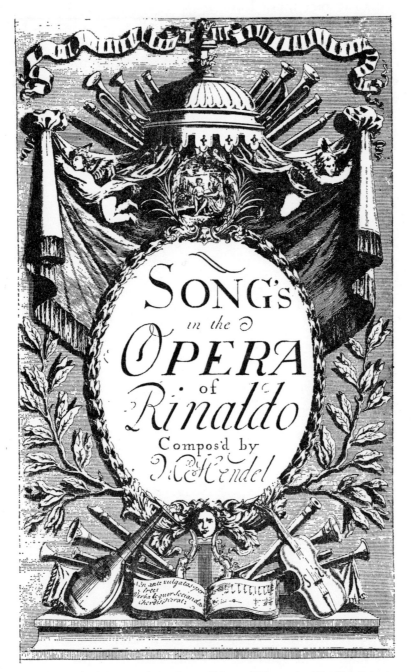

Figure 7. Title-page of the first edition of 'Songs in *Rinaldo*' (1711)

rearranged for it some music from *Agrippina* and his oratorios. The London audiences, who had never heard an opera half as good before, loved it. In one song, recorders were used to imitate birdsong, and live sparrows were released on the stage. In another, Handel, directing the performance (as composers generally did) from the harpsichord, accompanied in a brilliant style that astonished the audiences. And one of the songs, adapted from earlier works, is among the most beautiful he ever wrote.

Rinaldo: 'Lascia ch'io pianga'

The London opera season finished in June, and Handel hastened back to his duties in Hanover, again stopping at Düsseldorf on the way. Now life in Hanover must have seemed duller still. He was studying the English language, obviously with the idea of returning to London soon; and, after not much more than a year—during which he went to see his family in Halle— he obtained permission to go to England again. The first visit lasted about seven months, the second almost fifty years. From 1712 to the end of his life, London was Handel's home.

III

Settling in England

Handel had not been forgotten in London. *Rinaldo* had been given during the year he was away, and all was ready for him to write new operas now he was back. He composed two for the 1712–13 season, and soon after he wrote a Birthday Ode for Queen Anne—his first attempt at setting English words. He also wrote a sacred work in celebration of the Peace of Utrecht. In these he partly modelled his music on Purcell's, for Purcell had excelled in such works.

On his return he lived for a time as the guest of a friend. Then he was invited to stay at Burlington House in Piccadilly: the young Earl of Burlington was an enthusiastic supporter of the arts and literary men like Alexander Pope and John Gay were entertained there. (The house was on the site of the present Burlington House, now the home of the Royal Academy of Arts and Sciences.)

In 1714 Queen Anne died, and Handel's employer, the Elector of Hanover, was proclaimed George I of England. It used to be thought that George I was angry with Handel for staying away from his duties in Hanover so long. But probably he didn't particularly mind—he happily listened to music by Handel in his chapel a few days after his arrival in London, and he soon heard *Rinaldo* at the opera house. And he increased the generous annual payment to Handel which Queen Anne had made; it was increased again a few years later when Handel became harpsichord teacher to the royal princesses. The famous story of Handel's composing the *Water Music* to placate the king isn't true. Probably most of it was written for a party on the Thames in 1717. One of the London newspapers reported the event:

'On Wednesday [the 17th] Evening, at about 8, the King took Water at Whitehall in an open Barge . . . And went up the River towards Chelsea. Many other Barges with Persons of Quality attended, and so great a Number of Boats, that the whole River in a manner was cover'd; a City Company's Barge was employ'd for the Musick, wherein were 50 Instruments of all sorts, who play'd all the Way from Lambeth (while the Barges drove with the Tide without Rowing, as far as Chelsea) the finest Symphonies, compos'd express for this Occasion, by Mr. Hendel; which his Majesty liked so well, that he caus'd it to be plaid over three times in going and returning. At Eleven his Majesty went a-shore at Chelsea, where a Supper was prepar'd, and then there was another very fine Consort of Musick, which lasted till 2; after which, his Majesty came again into his Barge, and return'd the same Way, the Musick continuing to play till he landed.'

Another observer commented that the weather 'was all that could be desired for the festivity, the number of barges and above all of boats filled with people desirous of hearing was beyond counting'.

There are three groups of pieces altogether forming the *Water Music;* they may not all have been written for this particular occasion. The groups are in different keys, and have different characters; the longest group is in F, with horns, woodwind, and strings; there is a shorter, lighter group in G (major and minor), coloured by flutes and recorders; and a brilliant, ceremonious group in D, with trumpets. They consist mainly of movements in dance style—this was the usual thing for such works in those days, for the strong, clear rhythms made a good effect out of doors. Many French composers wrote in this way to entertain their royal family at sumptuous Versailles. On the opposite page are some of the melodies which Londoners living by the Thames might have heard one beautiful night in July 1717.

More compositions flowed from Handel's pen: two operas, and a Passion setting in German (see p. 22). This last may have been written during a brief visit to Germany in 1716—Handel travelled with the king and his retinue, who were going to Hanover. While in Germany he saw his mother, and gave help to the needy widow of his old teacher, Zachau.

When he returned to London he brought back with him an old friend from his university days, J. C. Schmidt, who became his secretary. Handel was busy at the opera house early in 1717, supervising revivals of two of his operas. Later that year he moved out to Edgware in Middlesex, where he lived as the guest of the Duke of Chandos. This notorious duke, who had been paymaster to the army and somehow managed to enrich himself by millions of pounds in the process, had built a palatial country house, called Cannons. He appointed the German composer Pepusch as head of his music and invited Handel to come and compose for him.

While at Cannons, or possibly at his new patron's town house, Handel composed his Chandos Anthems. Probably they were performed in the

Water Music: two movements

chapel at Cannons, or in the church lately built nearby (it is still there, unlike Cannons itself—the mansion was pulled down after some thirty years, and now there is a girls' school on the site).

Also written for Cannons were two dramatic works in English. One was a musical setting of the biblical story of Esther, at first called *Haman and Mordecai*; we shall come back to this later, under the title of *Esther*. In it Handel used a lot of the music he had originally composed for the Passion setting of 1716. The other work was wholly original. Called *Acis and Galatea*, it is a serenata or pastoral opera, much lighter and simpler in style than his Italian operas. Its story is the same one as Handel had used in the serenata composed in Naples, but this second version is much superior. It is one of Handel's freshest, most tuneful and immediately attractive works. The story is about the giant Polypheme, who comes across the shepherd Acis and the sea-nymph Galatea, who are in love; he kills Acis, whom Galatea, herself half goddess, transforms into a fountain.

Several of its songs are well known, particularly Polypheme's 'O ruddier than the cherry'. It has some fine choruses, especially the moving, elegiac ones after Acis's death. But probably the character of the work is best shown by a song like this one:

Acis and Galatea: 'As when the dove'

So far we have mentioned no instrumental music since the works of Handel's boyhood. About the time he was at Cannons he was composing for the harpsichord—including the movement named after the 'Harmonious Blacksmith of Edgware' (though in fact that character never existed, and was not even invented until a hundred years later!). Probably he wrote some sonatas for various instruments and continuo at this time, too, and possibly concertos as well. In 1720 he had his harpsichord suites published. This was partly because someone had got hold of an inaccurate copy and had them printed in Amsterdam (for which Handel was not paid—there was no proper law of copyright) and partly because it was generally considered that the royal family's harpsichord teacher should have written music for the instrument. A movement from one of the suites will be found on pages 30–1.

Meanwhile, opera in London was in abeyance, mainly through lack of money. But in 1719 a new venture was started: a commercial company to organize opera on a sounder basis. It was called the Royal Academy of Music. Many noblemen, including Burlington and Chandos, supported it, and the king promised a grant of £1000 a year. Handel was appointed musical director. His first job was to go to the continent and find some first-class singers—few English voices were up to the demands of the Italian opera style.

So off he went: Düsseldorf and Dresden were his main ports of call, and he engaged able singers at both places. Then he went to Halle to see his family; Bach, hearing of his presence nearby, travelled some twenty miles to see him, but on reaching Halle found that Handel had left. The two men never met. Handel arrived back in England late in 1719, eager to return to his first and strongest love, opera.

Gigue from suite for harpsichord (Book 2 No. 8)

IV

The Royal Academy

Before we go on to consider Handel's operas, it is worth going into
some of the differences between opera in those days and opera today.
Nowadays, an audience goes to an opera house to concentrate on
what happens on the stage, expecting it to be a dramatic as well as a musical
entertainment. In the early eighteenth century an opera performance was
also a social occasion. A member of the audience would rarely sit still in
his seat, watching and listening intently. Often he would talk to his neigh-
bours, or stroll out for a while if bored; he might have a meal, flirt, or even
play cards—for lights were left on during the performance.

If he wanted to, on his way in he could buy a book of words, with the
Italian printed on one page and an English translation opposite. With this
he could follow the action even if he didn't know a word of Italian (though
in fact most of the wealthy, cultured people who went to the opera would
have understood a certain amount).

But the main interest of the performance, for these audiences, lay in the
singing more than anything else. This was an age of great singers. The
composer and librettist were regarded as less important—in fact, it was
considered the composer's job, first of all, to provide music which demonstrated the voices to the best advantage. Often singers would carry around
their own favourite songs and insist on inserting them in different composers'
operas, even if they had no relevance to the story. Nearly all the opera stories
were taken from mythology or history, and were familiar to the audience.

The composer and librettist had to be careful to give each singer the right
number of songs in proportion to his or her importance. Most went to the
prima donna (leading lady), a soprano, and the *primo uomo* (leading man),
usually an alto or soprano. The leading male singer was usually a castrato,
a man whose voice had been prevented from breaking by an operation—
these men could sing in a high register with masculine power and, by all
accounts, great beauty. Lesser parts normally went to a second soprano and

The Florentine Court

A view of eighteenth-century London

a second male alto, or a woman contralto, and there was usually a bass role. Tenors were little used, and rarely for important parts.

There were very few duets or trios, and no true choruses at all in most operas. The dialogue between characters, and the action of the opera in general, took place in recitative, which is like ordinary speaking but at musical pitch. Recitative was mostly accompanied only by continuo, though at the most dramatic moments there was often a fuller orchestral accompaniment. The arias or songs, of which a full-length opera would have about thirty, were mostly in what is called 'da capo' form, meaning that the first part was repeated after the second (an A-B-A pattern). A good singer would be expected to embellish his music during the repeated part; the audiences judged him partly by the musicianship and vocal agility which he showed in doing this. After his song a singer normally left the stage, so that he could respond to the applause. All these conventions tended to damage the dramatic side of opera.

Nowadays, after two centuries of neglect, Handel's operas are beginning to be more often heard. They are not easy to give on the stage; they do not have the continuous dramatic impact for a modern audience that Mozart's or Verdi's, for example, do. But their music is too attractive, and too powerful, to be allowed to lie forgotten. Many of them have been broadcast, and a few recorded; and about thirty of his forty-odd have been given on the stage, in England or Germany, often by specialist groups. In England the castrato parts are generally sung by women, at the pitch Handel wrote them, but elsewhere they are usually transposed down an octave and sung by men.

The story of Handel's life in the next few years is little more than the story of opera. His whole life centred around the King's Theatre in the Haymarket (where today the Her Majesty's Theatre stands). He lived in what is now the West End of London, buying in 1723 a house in Brook Street—it is still there, the London office of a clothing manufacturer.

The Royal Academy of Music opened its doors in April 1720. Handel was in charge of the orchestra. An opera by the Italian composer Porta came first, then Handel's *Radamisto*, as the main event of the season: on its opening night there was so enormous a crowd that people had to struggle to get into the theatre.

During the summer opera was forgotten for a while because of the notorious South Sea Bubble. Handel was one of those to lose money in this financial crash, but he was not ruined by it. Before the Academy's second season opened, the managers invited a famous male singer, Senesino, to join the company, and they also brought to England another composer, Giovanni

Bononcini—Handel alone could not supply a sufficient number of new operas.

Figure 8. Giovanni Bononcini

So in the next few seasons the Academy performed operas by both composers, and also a few by Ariosti. Unfortunately, some unpleasant partisanship developed: some people proclaimed Handel's merits and would not hear of Bononcini's; others sang Bononcini's praises and decried Handel. The groups supporting the two composers even became associated with political factions. The king was a keen Handelian, so the party around him were too, while their opponents, including the Duke of Marlborough, were Bononcini men. One wit wrote of the dispute:

> *Some say, compar'd to Bononcini*
> *That Mynheer Handel's but a Ninny;*
> *Others aver, that he to Handel*
> *Is scarcely fit to hold a Candle:*
> *Strange all this Difference should be*
> *'Twixt Tweedle-dum and Tweedle-dee!*

Looking back now, we can see that Handel was the greater composer, but Bononcini had a graceful melodic gift and he knew how to show his singers' voices at their best. 1487046

Figure 9. Caricature of a scene from a Handel opera (probably *Flavio*); the singers (*left to right*) are Senesino, Cuzzoni and Berenstadt

Still, the composers' rivalry was child's play compared to the singers'. In 1723, the Academy managers engaged an Italian soprano, Cuzzoni, at a salary as absurdly high as a pop singer can earn today. She was a difficult person, obstinate and conceited: once Handel threatened to throw her out of the window if she went on refusing to sing what he had written for her. (She was not the only awkward one of Handel's singers. Once a tenor threatened to jump on the harpsichord if not allowed his own way. Handel is said to have replied: 'Let me know when, and I will advertise it, for more people will come to see you jump than to hear you sing'.) In 1726 another soprano was brought over, Faustina Bordoni, at an equally absurd salary. Of course, each had her supporters, and the supporters of the one found nothing to like in the other. Balanced judges thought Cuzzoni the more expressive, Faustina the more brilliant.

From the time of Faustina's arrival, the composers and their librettists had a diplomatic problem: the two ladies had to be given parts of exactly equal importance. Several of Handel's operas of this time have two soprano parts. He was particularly good at depicting female character in his music, and in *Admeto*, for example, he makes much of the contrast between the kind, noble Alcestis and the harsh, unscrupulous Antigone.

Of the thirteen operas Handel composed for the Academy, possibly the finest is *Giulio Cesare* (Julius Caesar). It tells the story of Caesar in Egypt, his meeting with Queen Cleopatra and her murderous brother, Ptolemy. Also in the opera are the widow and son of Cleopatra's Roman rival, Pompey. In one of the opera's most beautiful scenes Cleopatra, seeking to draw

Giulio Cesare: 'V'adoro, pupille'

rou-ses soft de-sires_____ , be-lov - ed, __ your glan - ces __ fly

swiftly home like Cupid's darts, a sin- gle look en - tran - ces and rou-ses soft de -

sires,_____ a sin - gle look en - tran - ces and rouses soft de -

sires.

Caesar to support her against Ptolemy, disguises herself as her own maid and tries to ensnare him with feminine charms.

Handel's only break from opera in the 1720s came in 1727. At the beginning of that year he became a British subject by naturalization. In the summer

Figure 10. The rival sopranos: Cuzzoni (*above*) and Faustina

The Royal Academy

George I died, and for George II's coronation Handel, now a Composer to the Chapel Royal, was commissioned to write four anthems for the coronation. One was the famous *Zadok the Priest*, played at every British coronation since.

By this time things were not going well at the opera house. During the performance in 1727 of a Bononcini opera (his last written for London) the Cuzzoni-Faustina quarrel, inflamed by cat-calls and hissing from unruly members of the audience, led to a 'most horrible and bloody battle' (as someone described it) between the two ladies. This took place on the stage— and with a member of the royal family in the audience.

In any case, the Academy was now rapidly running out of money. The public were no longer so keen on this extravagant and artificial novelty. Early in 1728, a satirical play with songs (all based on popular melodies) was put on at another theatre: called *The Beggar's Opera*, it poked fun at many features of life in London, among them the Italian opera. People who couldn't understand Italian, and who didn't like music as serious as Handel's, enjoyed it; so did quite a lot of others.

Handel wrote two new operas for production in 1728, but at the end of that season the money had run out. There was no hope of giving a 1728–9 season; Senesino, Cuzzoni and Faustina returned to Italy; and Handel had to think again about how he could get his operas performed.

V

Opera to Oratorio

Handel did not waste time merely thinking about his opera plans. By now he had a good deal of money invested, and still his regular income from the royal family. So he and Heidegger, as manager of the theatre, decided to organize opera seasons themselves.

Early in 1729 Handel, who had taken a five-year lease of the opera house, went off to the continent to find some new singers. He engaged six singers in Italy and a bass in Hamburg—where, no doubt, he found much to talk about with Telemann, now the leading figure in Hamburg's flourishing musical life. He also went further south, to Halle, where he saw his aged mother, now blind and infirm, for the last time. She died the next year. While he was in Halle Wilhelm Friedmann Bach, J. S. Bach's eldest son, called on him and presented an invitation to visit his father in Leipzig; but Handel could not spare the time to call there. In any case, he had no reason to go out of his way to meet a provincial Kapellmeister whose reputation was mainly local and whose music he may never have heard.

The new operas, staged in 1729 and 1730, were only mildly successful. To bring back the audiences Handel had to revive *Giulio Cesare*, always a favourite; in the next season he even put on *Rinaldo*, his first London opera, rewriting some of it to suit the new singers. His singers had not much impressed the opera-goers, so now he arranged for Senesino to return. The soprano was a lady called Strada del Pò, who had a fine voice but looked so poor on the stage that she was nicknamed 'The Pig'.

At one time, rather later, Handel's name and hers were linked in a way that suggested some sort of personal attachment (although she was in fact a married woman). Nothing is known at all of women he may have loved, or who may have loved him; there was a story about a singer to whom he was attracted during his time in Italy, and a young lady's name appears in a letter to Mattheson during his Hamburg days. Someone who probably knew him wrote that he was several times in love, but usually only for a short while, and always with women in the musical profession. A composer who could depict women in his music as vividly as Handel does is unlikely to have been entirely ignorant of them in real life.

While operas continued at the King's Theatre, Handel was also concerned with instrumental music. In 1733 and 1734 his London publishers brought out more harpsichord suites, some sonatas for one instrument and continuo (Op. 1), some for two instruments and continuo (Op. 2), and a set of six concertos (Op. 3).[1] The Op. 1 set, of twelve sonatas altogether, was divided between various instruments—two were meant for oboe, three for violin, three for flute, and four for recorder—though most of them could be played on any of the instruments. Here is a movement from a recorder sonata:

Recorder Sonata, Op. 1 No. 7: Gavotte

[1] Opus numbers were usually given at this time only to works like groups of sonatas collected for publication; 'Op. 1' did not of course signify that these were his first compositions.

In 1732 several things happened to take Handel's mind off opera. On his forty-seventh birthday, a concert was given, as part of a regular series, at a tavern in London's Strand. The programme consisted of just one work:

43

Handel's *Esther*. The organizer of the concert was a Handel enthusiast who had come across copies of *Esther* and felt that it was worth reviving after some dozen years' neglect.

Handel was probably present at this performance, largely an amateur one. But then a group of professionals got hold of *Esther*, too, and advertised a performance of it. Handel couldn't sit by and let his professional rivals make money out of his music. But there was no copyright law to protect him. So now he decided to put on performances himself, at the opera house, adding some new items. Probably he intended it to be staged, as a sort of sacred opera, but the church authorities banned the staging of a work on a sacred subject.

Next, much the same thing happened with *Acis and Galatea*. It was given, as an opera, by some of Handel's rivals; he then put on performances him-self—again adding a lot of other music. This time he drew on his Italian setting of the same story, partly so that the Italian singers could sing in their own language. Their attempts at English in *Esther* had been laughable: some years later, at a performance of *Esther*, an Italian sang 'I come, my Queen, to chaste delights'—which to the audience sounded like 'I comb my Queen to chase the lice.'

All the same, these happenings sowed in Handel's mind the seeds of an idea about performing dramatic works in the English language. Not English opera—the idea never really caught his interest—but oratorio. We shall later see that these seeds took almost ten years to germinate fully. For the moment he produced two more oratorios. One of them, *Deborah*, he gave in the opera house, with almost a hundred performers, a huge number for those days. The choir was about twenty-five, the orchestra more than seventy. When nowadays we give massive performances of Handel, it's worth noting that he himself used almost three times as many players as singers—and that a performance on this scale was considered 'excessive noisy' by at least some listeners (one actually wrote those words in his diary).

Much of the music of *Deborah* was adapted by Handel from earlier works. His next oratorio, *Athalia*, was composed for performance in summer 1733 at Oxford. Handel may have been invited to become an honorary doctor of music at Oxford University, although he never actually did so. But he went to Oxford with a large company of musicians, and gave a series of pro-grammes there. Some members of the university disapproved of such goings-on; one of them made a bad-tempered entry in his diary about 'Handel and (his lowsy Crew) a great number of foreign fidlers'.

Athalia tells the biblical story of a tyrant, usurping queen of the Jews who

Lordſhips appointed ſeveral Lieutenants to his Majeſty's Ships that are to conduct his Majeſty to Holland; and the Durſley Galley is to go afterwards to Newfoundland.

Yeſterday *South Sea Stock* was 99, 99 1 8th, to 1 4ths. *South Sea Annuity* 110 to 1 8·h. *South Sea Bonds* 2 l. 12 s. *Bank* 148 1 half to 5 8·h. *Bank Circulation* 7 l. 5 s. *Million Bank* 112. *India* 177 3 4ths, 178 1 half, 178 1 4th. *India Bonds* 6 l. 6 s. *Royal Aſſurance* 99 3 4ths. *London Aſſurance* 13 1 half. *York Buildings* 7 1 half. *African* 42. *Three per Cent. Annuity* 97 1 4th to 3 8ths. *Engliſh Copper* 2 l. 10 s. *Welſh Copper* 1 l. 17 s. *Three 1 half per Cent.* 3 Prem.

By His MAJESTY's COMMAND.

AT the KING's THEATRE in the HAY-MARKET, on Tueſday the 2d Day of May, will be performed,

The SACRED STORY of ESTHER:

AN

ORATORIO in ENGLISH.

Formerly compoſed by Mr. HANDEL, and now reviſed by him, with ſeveral Additions, and to be performed by a great Number of the beſt Voices and Inſtruments.

N. B. There will be no Action on the Stage, but the Houſe will be fitted up in a decent Manner, for the Audience. The Muſick to be diſpoſed after the Manner of the Coronation Service.

Tickets will be delivered at the Office in the Opera houſe, at the uſual Prices.

Never Perform'd in Publick before,

AT the Great Room in Villars-ſtreet YORK-Buildings, To-morrow, being Thurſday the 20th of this Inſtant April, will be perfo'm'd,

ESTHER an ORATORIO:

OR,

SACRED DRAMA.

As it was compos'd originally for the moſt noble James Duke of Chandos, the Words by Mr. POPE, and the Muſick by Mr. HANDEL.

Tickets to be had at the Place of Performance at 5 s. each.

To begin exactly at 7 o'Clock.

Figure 11. The rival advertisements in *The Daily Journal*, 19 April 1732

is overthrown. It contains some strongly dramatic music. But one of its most beautiful songs is for the foster-mother of the boy who is the rightful king, when she learns that the cruel Athalia intends to kill the child she has tended.

Athalia: 'Faithful cares'

well, bea - my dawn of joy fare - well, bea - my dawn of

joy fare-well! Faith-ful cares of joy ex-tend - ed, love - ly

hopes for - ev - er end - ed, love - ly hopes for - ev - er end - ed, bea - my

dawn of joy fare - well, bea - my dawn of joy fare - well, fare - well,____

bea - my dawn, bea - my dawn of joy, fare-well!

When Handel came back to London from Oxford he found an unpleasant situation brewing. His latest opera, *Orlando*, had been successful (as it deserved, for it was among his most imaginative). But people were beginning to resent Handel's dominating position in London's operatic life. Although he was recognized all over Europe as one of the greatest composers of the day, his gruff manner had made him some powerful enemies. And he had become extremely unpopular by raising the ticket prices for performances of *Deborah*. This happened at just the same time as the Prime Minister, Sir Robert Walpole, tried to introduce a bill imposing heavy tobacco taxes.

The result of all this was that a group of wealthy noblemen got together to found an opera organization in rivalry to Handel's. The Prince of Wales—always keen to oppose his father, a Handel supporter—was a leading spirit. This organization, generally called 'The Nobility Opera', engaged all Handel's singers except the loyal Strada; they sent to Italy for the soprano Cuzzoni and for Farinelli, the most famous of all the castrato singers.

48

Admission ticket to a performance of
Samson in 1752

Frontispiece to the first edition of
Tamerlano

Handel's watch, by Golling of Augsburg

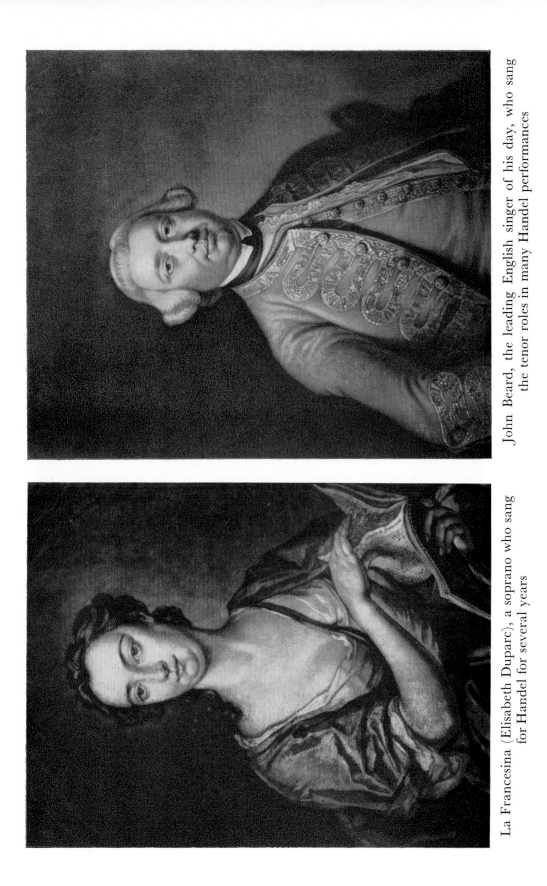

La Francesina (Elisabeth Duparc), a soprano who sang for Handel for several years

John Beard, the leading English singer of his day, who sang the tenor roles in many Handel performances

We might have expected Handel to turn to oratorio for good in these circumstances; but in fact he put it aside for a time and concentrated on fighting off this challenge to his position as London's leading opera composer.

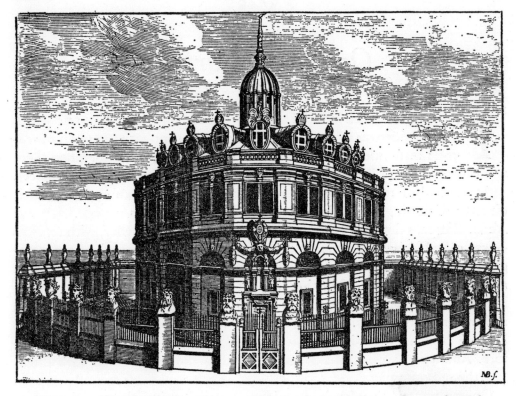

Figure 12. The Sheldonian Theatre, Oxford, where *Athalia* was first performed

VI

Operatic Warfare

The battle between Handel and his operatic opponents was one which neither side was likely to win. There were simply not enough opera-goers in London to support two opera houses; after all, when there was only one opera house, it had failed through lack of regular audiences.

At the end of 1733 the Nobility Opera opened, with an opera by their director of music, the Italian composer Porpora. It was called *Arianna in Nasso*. Handel's first new opera—his season had opened earlier, with revivals—was called *Arianna in Creta*; it dealt with a different part of the mythological story of the same Ariadne. The London public didn't get enthusiastic about either Ariadne: often the king sat in the half-empty theatre in the Haymarket, while about a mile away his son sat in the half-empty theatre at Lincoln's Inn Fields. One movement from Handel's opera, though, did become popular, the minuet which formed the third movement of its overture. Amateur harpsichordists could buy it, arranged for their instrument (see the opposite page).

Operas paused in March. London was celebrating the marriage of a princess; for the occasion Handel not only supplied a wedding anthem but also wrote a special serenata, drawing on *Athalia* for most of its music.

At the end of the season his lease of the theatre expired. Heidegger now broke his long association with Handel and leased the opera house to the Nobility Opera. So Handel promptly arranged to present his operas at the Theatre-Royal, Covent Garden. During the summer he went to the fashionable spa of Tunbridge Wells, to take the waters. And he started work on his next opera; on his return he played over some of it to the king, who, according to a newspaper columnist, 'express'd great Satisfaction with the Composition'.

This season, 1734–5, both opera houses made still greater efforts to draw in the public. By now Farinelli had arrived to reinforce the Nobility Opera's singers. One writer said of him: 'Imagine Senesino's art combined with

Arianna: minuet from the overture[1]

[1] This example is photographed from a contemporary copy of an arrangement for harpsichord. The copy belonged to a player who liked to write in embellishments to the melody, and figures over the bass to suggest extra harmony.

Operatic Warfare

Carestini's [Handel's principal singer], and a voice more beautiful than those two together'. Another wrote: 'He was a revelation ... until hearing him I had heard only a fraction of what human song can achieve'. Handel had engaged a troupe of French ballet dancers, and his operas for this season include some attractive ballet scenes. The last of them was *Alcina*, one of the richest of all his operas. It is the story of a sorceress, Alcina, who ensnares Ruggiero until he is rescued by the courage of the woman who truly loves him. As Ruggiero leaves Alcina's enchanted meadows, he bids them farewell in this moving music.

Alcina : 'Verdi prati'

52

ci - na's pow'r has fal - ter'd———, to a des - ert cold and grey,

to a de - sert cold and grey, Ver - dant pas-tures, glades so charming,

all your beau-ties soon will de-cay. . all your beau-ties soon will de-cay.

In spite of *Alcina's* merit, the opera season went badly. Handel decided not to put on operas at all in the autumn of 1735. The early part of the next year, however, saw two new works. One was a setting of an ode in praise of music, *Alexander's Feast*, of which the words were largely by Dryden. Written for concert performance, not staging, it is full of happy ideas and has some splendid choral writing. The public took to it at once. The other new piece was a festive opera written in celebration of the Prince of Wales's marriage.

That autumn he started on operas again, still in competition with the Nobility Opera. In the 1736–7 season he wrote three new operas, none of them anywhere near his highest level. By the end of the season both Handel and his rivals had lost a great deal of money. The frightful strain of these years had told on him. He had some kind of paralytic stroke, and mentally too he was off balance.

But he was not a man to be laid low for long. In the summer he went to the spa at Aix-la-Chapelle (Aachen) and tackled the cures with such determination that he emerged, completely restored to health, so quickly that the nuns in attendance there thought a miracle had occurred.

He was not cured of the desire to compose operas. Heidegger was still organizing some performances at the King's Theatre, and on his return

AT the KING's THEATRE in the HAY-MARKET, this prefent Saturday, being the 25th Day of January, will be perform'd a new Opera, call'd

A R I A D N E.

Pit and Boxes to be put together, and no Perfons to be admitted without Tickets, which will be delivered this Day, at the Office in the Hay-Market, at Half a Guinea each.

GALLERY FIVE SHILLINGS.

By His MAJESTY's COMMAND,

No Perfons whatever to be admitted behind the SCENES.
To begin at Six o'Clock.

Not Acted this Season.

By the Company of Comedians,

AT the Theatre-Royal in COVENT-GARDEN, this prefent Saturday, being the 26th Day of January, will be prefented a Comedy, call'd

Æ S O P.

Written by the late Sir JOHN VANBRUGH.

Figure 13. Advertisement in *The Daily Journal*, 26 January 1734

Handel promptly arranged to write two for the 1737–8 season. That season was interrupted when the Queen died. She had been a good friend to Handel; the funeral anthem he wrote was no mere formal tribute. The second of Handel's operas for this season was *Serse*, the one for which he wrote the so-called Largo. It is actually marked 'Larghetto', and is sung by the weary King Xerxes as he settles down for a rest in a shady spot—the words, beginning 'Ombra mai fù', are in praise of the tree which provides the shade (see figure 14, p. 55).

Handel's recovery of health and spirits, and the ending of the foolish operatic rivalries, helped to bring him back into public favour. Everyone now seemed to realize that Handel was something more than just another composer, and he began to be treated with something more like the respect due to genius. His audiences were good, and a reporter wrote that, on his reappearance in public, Handel was 'honour'd with extraordinary and repeated Signs of Approbation'. One particular 'sign of approbation' was the erection of a statue of him at Vauxhall, the famous public pleasure

Figure 14. The manuscript of 'Ombra mai fù' from *Serse*—known as 'Handel's Largo'

garden by the Thames where rich and poor, young and old, alike came to enjoy themselves in a variety of ways during the summer evenings. Music was played there regularly, and a newspaper commented on the appropriateness of having Handel's statue in the place where his music had 'so often charm'd even the greatest Crouds into the profoundest Calm and most decent Behaviour'. The statue, done for the art-loving proprietor of Vauxhall, Jonathan Tyers, by the French sculptor Roubillac, can be seen today in the Victoria and Albert Museum.

Handel's next major composition, on which he started work in the summer of 1738, was a new oratorio. Three years back, a wealthy amateur poet, Charles Jennens, who for a long time had admired Handel's music, had sent him an oratorio libretto. The subject was the story of Saul and his envy of the young David. Handel's interest was fired by the dramatic qualities in the text.

55

While he was working on it, Jennens called on him, and found his mind still in a slightly disturbed state. 'Mr. Handel's head is more full of maggots than ever', he wrote to a friend. Three of the 'maggots'—which we would call 'bees in his bonnet'—were ideas about the new oratorio. One was a chorus he wanted to add at the end, rather pointlessly (he later removed it). Another was about a new sort of organ he wanted to have built, from which he could see the performers better so that he need not beat time. (Conductors of the modern kind were almost unknown; performances were directed by the keyboard player and the leading violinist.) And the third concerned a set of bells operated from a keyboard. This last was for the festive scene at the beginning of *Saul*, when the conquering David is welcomed home with peals of bells.

Saul: Carillon Symphony

Saul begins with a series of movements, in which that passage comes, in celebration of the Israelites' victory. The oratorio ends with an Elegy after their later defeat by the Philistines, in which the deaths of Saul and Jonathan are mourned. The famous Dead March comes at this point. In between, Handel gives a vivid musical picture of Saul's growing envy and hatred of David. The chorus, who act sometimes as the Israelites and sometimes just as observers of the action, have two particularly fine movements in which they comment on the evils of envy and rage. And there is an eerie scene where Saul consults the Witch of Endor and summons up the dead Samuel's spirit to advise him.

Saul was performed at the beginning of 1739, starting off what was Handel's first true oratorio season. Later in the season he gave another new oratorio, *Israel in Egypt*. But that, with little solo music, was less successful—the audiences still loved fine singing. Although its magnificent choral writing has since made the work popular, in Handel's day it never did well.

Handel himself did not compose all the music of *Israel in Egypt*. We have already seen that he often 'borrowed' from his earlier works when composing in a hurry: sometimes he used the same song over again with little or no alteration, apart from making sure that the new words would fit; sometimes he just took a phrase from a melody and based a new piece on it. But from about 1737 onwards—the time of his breakdown in health—he borrowed from other composers too. Much of *Israel in Egypt* is taken from a work by an obscure Italian, Erba. He also drew on Telemann, Muffat and many other composers, German and Italian.

This borrowing—without permission or acknowledgement, of course—may seem to us faintly dishonest. To Handel it probably didn't. Not many people knew about it; one who did, the gifted English composer, William Boyce, wrote: 'He takes pebbles and converts them into diamonds'. It's true that the changes he made in other men's music were always vast improvements. In these difficult years he clearly often found it hard to get a composition started, and it seems that he used ideas by other composers as 'stepping-stones', as a sort of stimulation to his own inventiveness. This applied particularly in instrumental works. When there were words to set, their character and rhythm often gave him the ideas he needed.

But the concertos he published about this time are among his sturdiest and freshest music. During the intervals of oratorio performances, since 1733, Handel had entertained his audiences with instrumental items, usually concertos, mostly organ concertos in which he played the solo part himself. His brilliant organ playing—often he improvised (made the music up as he went along)—became as much of an attraction as the singing.

In 1738 he put together a collection of six organ concertos, for publication. Some of them were arranged from other works, including music written almost thirty years before, and one of them is a rather slapdash version of a recorder sonata. The idea of a concerto for keyboard instrument and orchestra was still new in Handel's day; Bach, in Leipzig, composed some for harpsichord at much the same time, and he too drew on works he had written earlier. Handel's set of concertos shows a variety of ingenious and

The figure's odd_ yet who would think?
(Within this Tunn of Meat & Drink)
There dwells the Soul of soft Desires,
And all that HARMONY inspires:

THE
Charming
BRUTE,

Can Contrast such as this be found?
Upon the Globe's extensive Round:
There can_ you Hoglhead is his Seat,
His sole Devotion is _ to Eat.

Pub. according to Act of Parliam.ᵗ March 26 1754

Figure 15. 'The Charming Brute', Goupy's notorious caricature of Handel

happy ways of using the organ and orchestra together. They are as suitable for the harpsichord as the organ, and were published as concertos for either instrument. This meant that the many people who made music at home could play them with just a harpsichord, a couple of violins and a cello. On the next page is an extract from the fourth concerto.

Organ Concerto, Op. 4 No. 4: opening of first movement

etc.

VII

The Masterpieces

Most of the music by which Handel is remembered nowadays was composed in the years we have just come to—1739 to 1742. 1739 was the year of *Israel in Egypt*, 1741 saw the composition of *Messiah* and *Samson*. This was a marvellously fertile spell, and within it there were shorter periods when inspired music flowed from his pen at an astonishing speed.

One of these periods came in the autumn of 1739. First came an Ode for St. Cecilia's Day, three-quarters of an hour's music; it was put on paper in ten days. Then, immediately, he started work on a set of concertos. He wrote a dozen in about five weeks. (Composers of the early eighteenth century nearly always published their works in sets of six or twelve; it was much more convenient for amateurs to buy them like that rather than singly, and also cheaper to print that way.)

These concertos, which were published the next spring and are known as his Opus 6, are of the 'concerto grosso' type. They are written for strings, optional oboes and continuo, with solo parts for two violins and cello. This was the sort of concerto which Corelli had composed, some thirty years earlier, and which many other Italians had used. Handel and his publisher called them by an English title, 'Twelve Grand Concertos'.

Handel's Opus 6 concertos are extraordinarily varied, with fugues, song-like movements, and dances side by side. In some there are important solo parts, in others the soloists simply play as part of the orchestra. All of them are tuneful, all are grand and spacious, and all are full of new, fanciful ideas. A short movement from one of them is on the opposite page.

Handel published these concertos 'by subscription'—meaning that he invited purchasers to put their names down in advance (by doing so they probably got the music more cheaply). They also had the privilege of having their names printed in the front; and by looking at this list of subscribers' names we can see who some of the purchasers were. At the head of

Concerto, Op. 6 No. 3: finale

the list are six members of the royal family (regular patrons of Handel), followed by various noblemen, several composers, acquaintances like Charles Jennens, and the proprietors of Vauxhall Gardens and the Covent Garden theatre. There were also musical societies all over the British Isles—Canterbury, Lincoln, Oxford, Salisbury, Dublin—and in London, for example the 'Monday Night Musical Society at ye Globe Tavern, Fleet St.'. Nobody who cared for music would want to be without the Great Mr. Handel's latest concertos!

Figure 16. The first page of Handel's Op. 6 'Grand Concertos' (solo violin part)

Gustavus Waltz, a bass who sang in Handel's oratorios; he was said to be Handel's cook

Susanna Cibber, an actress and mezzo-soprano, sister of the composer Thomas Arne, who sang in the first performance of *Messiah*

Thomas Hudson's famous portrait of Handel with the score of *Messiah* before him

The 1739–40 concert season was spoilt by two things. First, the country was at war, with Spain; second, there was a long and bitter frost in London —the Thames froze solid, so solid that shops and printing presses could be set up on the ice, and oxen roasted over fires. It was impossible to keep the theatre warm enough, and performances came to a stop when the new Ode had been heard only three times.

Handel did not sit idle. He had been sent a new libretto by Jennens, an adaptation of Milton's poem *L'Allegro ed il Penseroso* ('The cheerful man and the pensive man') with some additions of his own. Handel was always stimulated by really first-class verse. Milton's poem is not dramatic, but it is richly descriptive, most of all of the natural beauty of the English country-side and of carefree country people. Handel responded with fresh, gay music, sometimes very like Purcell, quite like his own *Acis and Galatea*. The simple, melodious manner of the song on pp. 66–7 also resembles that of the music by Handel's friends among English composers, Boyce and Arne for example.

Not even *L'Allegro* could bring the crowds to the theatre. An anonymous amateur poet commented:

> *If e'er* Arion's *music calm'd the floods,*
> *And* Orpheus *ever drew the dancing woods;*
> *Why do not* British *trees and forest throng*
> *To hear the sweeter notes of* Handel's *song?*

In the 1740–1 season Handel made a last attempt to return to opera. He looked out the score of *Imeneo*, which he had started more than two years before but then put aside. When that was finished he wrote another, *Deidamia*. But *Imeneo* had a mere two performances, *Deidamia* three. When the curtain went down on February 10, 1741, Handel's operatic career came to an end. Apart from one or two revivals in the following years, it was another two centuries before a Handel opera was again seen on the London stage.

Rumours circulated that Handel, whose oratorio performances too had failed to attract audiences, was so disgusted with the English public that he was about to leave the country, perhaps for ever. Possibly he thought of doing so: he cannot have been happy to perform to empty theatres.

Handel did leave London. But it was for only one season. And he did not leave the British Isles. Early in 1741 he had received a letter from the Lord Lieutenant of Ireland, inviting him to go to Dublin and give concerts in aid of various charities there. Dublin was the only place in the British Isles besides London where there was a court; the Lord Lieutenant was the king's

E

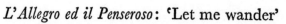

L'Allegro ed il Penseroso: 'Let me wander'

land, now the milk - maid sing - eth blithe, and the

mow - er whets his scythe, and e - ver - y shep - herd tells his tale; un - der the haw-thorn, in the

dale, and e - ver - y shep - herd tells his tale, un - der the

haw - thorn in the dale.

representative, and he lived in comparable splendour. So there was likely to be a larger number of wealthy people, and music-lovers, in Dublin than in any other city outside London. And, if there was a large gulf in England between the living standards of rich and poor, in Dublin it was far worse. The richer people, aware of this, gave generously to the city's many charitable institutions, especially hospitals for the poor.

So, with a trip to Dublin in mind, Handel settled down to prepare the music he would take with him. He took several of his major works in English—*L'Allegro, Acis, Alexander's Feast, Saul*, and *Esther*—and, probably with the Dublin performances in mind, he wrote a new oratorio, one quite unlike anything he had done before. It was generally called 'The Sacred Oratorio', or, simply, *Messiah*.

On the way to Dublin Handel stopped at Chester, where he astonished the local people with his brilliant playing on the cathedral organ and tried over, with some singers, parts of his new oratorio. A music-loving schoolboy called Charles Burney, who later became a distinguished musician and writer on music, attended one of these rehearsals. He saw Handel spluttering with rage because the bass, a printer by trade, could not manage to sight-read his part.

In November 1741 Handel arrived in Dublin. First he gave a series of six oratorio performances, which thrilled the Dubliners, not used to so high a standard. The *Dublin Journal* reported:

'Last Wednesday Mr. Handell had his first Oratorio, at Mr. Neal's Musick Hall in Fishamble-Street, which was crowded with a more numerous and polite Audience than ever was seen upon the like Occasion. The Performance was superior to any Thing of the Kind in this Kingdom before; and our Nobility and Gentry to show their Taste for all Kinds of Genius, expressed their great Satisfaction, and have already given all imaginable Encouragement to this grand Musick.'

Handel was delighted by this overdue success, as his cheerful letter to Jennens, back in London, shows:

'the Performance was received with a general Approbation . . . the Musick sounds delightfully in this charming Room, which puts me in such Spirits (and my Health being so good) that I exert my self on my Organ with more than usual Success.'

This letter also shows that he had at last put opera behind him, for he mentions that he had heard with amusement how unsuccessful were the operas then being given in London. 'The first Opera I heard my Self before I left London, and it made me very merry all along my journey', he wrote.

The Masterpieces

On April 13, 1742 came the climax of the Dublin visit: the first performance of *Messiah*. Seven hundred people were crammed into a hall designed for six hundred; ladies had been asked to come without the usual hoops in their skirts, and gentlemen without their swords, to make extra space. This is how the event was reported:

'On Tuesday last Mr. Handel's Sacred Grand Oratorio, the *MESSIAH*, was performed at the New Musick-Hall in Fishamble-street; the best Judges allowed it to be the most finished piece of Musick. Words are wanting to express the exquisite Delight it afforded to the admiring crouded Audience. The Sublime, the Grand, and the Tender, adapted to the most elevated, majestick and moving Words, conspired to transport and charm the ravished Heart and Ear. It is but Justice to Mr. Handel that the World should know, he generously gave the Money arising from this Grand Performance, to be equally shared by the Society for relieving Prisoners, the Charitable Infirmary, and Mercer's Hospital, for which they will ever gratefully remember his Name.'

For *Messiah*, like his other Dublin concerts, Handel used the choir that sang in the two cathedrals (St. Patrick's and Christ Church) and two women soloists from London, including Susanna Cibber, sister of the composer Arne. Probably the total number of performers was about forty. *Messiah* is usually thought of as Handel's masterpiece, and certainly it is one of the most steadily inspired of his works. Handel was, up to a point, a religious man— in his last years he worshipped twice every day at a church near his home (St. George's, Hanover Square). While composing the 'Hallelujah' chorus, he once said, it was 'as if I saw God on his throne, and all his angels around him'; but then, as a dramatic composer, he always visualized any scene he was writing. The music of *Messiah*, like so much of Handel's, is a blend of different styles: English church music (especially the choruses), the German Passion-music tradition, the Italian melodic style (in fact three of the choruses are arranged from Italian love-duets which Handel had written thirty years before). No examples from *Messiah* are given here as the opportunities to hear its music are so frequent.

After a few more performances in Dublin, Handel left for London during August. He intended to return, for he had enjoyed his nine months there: he had made many friends, and his performances had been marvellously successful. But probably he was glad, as anybody is after being away, to return to his home city and be driven up Brook Street to his own house.

VIII

Oratorios in London

In Dublin, Handel had given most of his performances 'by subscription': that is, he sold tickets for the entire series at a slightly reduced rate. This method, used by most musical societies of the time, had many advantages, particularly in ensuring a regular audience. So he decided to try it in London with his oratorio performances at Covent Garden. On his return he may have been momentarily tempted to return to opera; he had an extremely generous offer from one of his former enemies to write or arrange some new ones, but eventually turned it down.

Before going to Dublin Handel had drafted out a new oratorio, *Samson*, and after putting the finishing touches to the work he used it to open his subscription season. *Samson* has many 'borrowings', from Telemann and others, but it has a good deal that is typical Handel, especially in the second of its three acts. Here the Israelite hero, blind and in chains, first repulses the approaches of the traitorous Dalila and then treats the taunts of the boasting Philistine warrior, Harapha, with due contempt. The destruction of the Philistine banqueting hall, and the death of Samson, are also powerfully portrayed. Perhaps the most moving song is in Act 1, where Samson sings in despair of his blindness (see pp. 71–3).

Samson was well received by the Londoners, who had not heard much of Handel for the previous year and a half. Crowds were turned away at the doors. Then he introduced *Messiah* to London. Musically it was liked, but in certain religious circles the idea of singing biblical words in a theatre was disapproved, even more so than it had been in the case of *Israel in Egypt*. One man wrote to a newspaper asking 'if the *Playhouse* is a fit *Temple* . . . or a Company of *Players* fit *Ministers* of *God's Word*'. So *Messiah* made only slow progress at first in public taste; but before long such prejudices were overcome, and it eventually became by far the most popular of Handel's oratorios. Over the next few years he came to use it at the end of each oratorio season.

Samson: 'Total eclipse'

wel - come day! To - tal e - clipse! no sun, no moon, all

dark,_____ a-midst the blaze of noon! Why thus de-priv'd Thy prime de-cree?

sun, moon, and stars, are dark to me. sun, moon, and stars, sun, moon, and stars, are

dark to me. sun, moon, and stars, sun, moon, and stars___ are dark to

me!

In the spring of 1743 Handel had another paralytic stroke, but it was a mild one and did not stop him from having a busy, productive summer. (He always preferred to compose in the summers, when the days were long and the light good.) During a spell of four months he wrote *Semele*, a Te Deum and anthem to commemorate the battle of Dettingen, where George II himself had led the British armies to victory, and another biblical oratorio, on the story of Joseph.

This last, to a poor libretto, is one of Handel's least interesting oratorios, and the Dettingen work was mainly pieced together from music by a composer called Urio. But *Semele* is one of his most beautiful works. The words were adapted from Congreve; and once again Handel showed how much the quality of the text affected the quality of his music. The story is the classical one of Semele, daughter of King Cadmus of Thebes, who is whisked off to Olympus when on the point of marriage because she and Jupiter, king of the gods, are in love. Jupiter's wife Juno is naturally angry and jealous, and conspires against Semele. Handel was always good at portraying jealousy and anger in his music.

But *Semele* is most of all lovable for the sheer melodic charm of its songs— though later it becomes dramatic when Juno's plot succeeds and Semele causes herself to be destroyed by one of Jupiter's thunderbolts. The second act, which includes the song 'Where'er you walk', is a succession of beautiful items. One of the most attractive and typical pieces in the work is the gavotte-like song which Semele sings on her arrival on Olympus, to reassure her family and the people of Thebes that she is happy (see pp. 74–5).

Semele opened Handel's 1744 subscription season, but was no great success. Probably the audiences felt that it was an uneasy mixture—an opera-like story, but with oratorio-like choruses, and not (of course) given as a stage work. And the kind of audience Handel was now beginning to attract was drawn from the professional and merchant classes instead of just the wealthy and cultured 'nobility and gentry'. These were people with less experienced judgement on what was good or bad art, and they liked to have their religious

Semele: 'Endless pleasure'

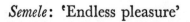

Moderately fast

End - less pleas - ure,   end - less pleas - ure, end - less   love, Sem - e -

le en - joys a - bove,   end - less love,   end - less

love, end-less plea - - - -

- - - - - - -sure, end-less love, Se - me - le en - joys a -

bove _____ Se - me -

le en-joys a - bove.

etc.

feelings affected by going to an oratorio. *Semele* certainly could not do that, as the biblical oratorios could.

Joseph followed *Semele* at the theatre but was not much more successful. Handel was said to have been 'mightily out of humour' at the rehearsals because of the incompetent singers. This was something that happened quite often. Charles Burney, who later sang and played under him, told how Handel once raged at him when he made a mistake, 'a circumstance very terrific to a young musician'. But when Handel found that his mistake was caused by a copying error, he apologized generously ('I pec your barton —I am a very odd tog', he was quoted as saying by Burney, who tried to reproduce his German accent).

There are other stories of Handel's rehearsals. At one time he held them in Carlton House, home of the Prince of Wales. Handel became angry if there were interruptions, even from the royal family themselves. According to Burney, 'if the maids of honour, or any other female attendants, talked, during the performance, I fear that [Handel], not only swore, but called names; yet, at such times, the princess of Wales, with her accustomed mild-ness and benignity, used to say, "Hush! hush! Handel's in a passion." '

In the 1744–5 season Handel moved back to the Haymarket (opera, yet again, had collapsed). This time he planned to give twenty-four perform-ances. He was too optimistic. Once more he found himself giving perform-ances to half-empty houses. At first he decided to break off the season after a mere six performances, but a letter to the leading London newspaper rallied his supporters and eventually he was able to give sixteen. He did not try the subscription system again.

This season there were again two new works, and again one of them was not a true oratorio. Like *Semele*, *Hercules* was based on a classical story— about the hero's return to his home, his wife's jealousy, and his death. And again the public did not take to it. Handel must have been puzzled and saddened to see the failure of these two works, which seem to us (and prob-ably did to him) to be among his most original and most inspired.

The other novelty of this season was *Belshazzar*. Jennens supplied the libretto, which impressed Handel: 'a Noble Piece, very grand and un-common', he called it. It tells the story of Belshazzar, Daniel's interpretation of the writing on the wall, and Babylon's downfall. Belshazzar's mother, Nitocris, plays an important part (her recitative at the start of the oratorio is shown on p. 78, as it appears in the edition published just after the first performance).

In this oratorio, as in most of them, Handel tries to use music to help us

76

understand the characters and emotions of the people involved. In many oratorios he extends this to the choruses. *Belshazzar* has three different groups —the captive Israelites, the Persians who conquer Babylon, and the Babylonians themselves; and Handel is very careful to give them different sorts of music. The Persians, naturally, have generally vigorous choruses. Most of the Israelite choruses are solemn and imposing, and several are elaborate fugues. For the gay, pleasure-loving Babylonians he writes tuneful and rhythmic music—in fact in all his oratorios the pagan or heathen people seem to have the liveliest tunes. This is how one of the Babylonian choruses starts:

Belshazzar: 'Ye tutelar gods'

During the summer of 1745, Bonnie Prince Charlie landed in Scotland and marched south with the rebel Jacobite forces to overthrow George II. This caused a good deal of alarm in London; it affected ordinary people much more than the wars with Spain and France had done. In December they reached Derby, but then began to retreat before the government armies. It was during this time that the national anthem became accepted (nobody knows its composer for certain). Patriotic music was wanted. When Handel started his next oratorio season, early in 1746, he produced for the occasion his *Occasional Oratorio*, to biblical words in praise of the people fighting for liberty. Much of the music is drawn from his earlier works.

Otherwise 1746 was a quiet year for Handel; apart from directing the three performances of the *Occasional Oratorio*, he appeared little in public. But his music continued to be heard, not only in England and Ireland, but also on the Continent—a newly formed German Society of Musical Science elected him their first and only honorary member during the year. In the summer, after a spell of illness, he started making plans for the next season, and on the Prince of Wales's recommendation visited the Rev. Thomas Morell. With Morell as his librettist he embarked on the final stage of his composing career.

Figure 17. From the first edition of *Belshazzar*

IX

The Last Years

With the public jubilant about the victory over the Jacobite rebellion, Handel set out in his next oratorio to provide music to suit their mood. The result was *Judas Maccabaeus*, which he dedicated to the victor at Culloden, the cruel Duke of Cumberland.

Judas Maccabaeus was an enormous success when it had its first performance in April 1747. It was so popular that in later seasons Handel revived it far more often than any other of his oratorios. Looking at it now, it is easy to see why it was popular, for it is full of good melody. But it is less subtle than most of his oratorios in its style and drama. The following song is a good example of the kind of stirring music Handel provided.

Judas Maccabaeus: 'Sound an alarm'

Handel and Morell were naturally anxious to repeat *Judas's* success. The story of the next oratorio, *Alexander Balus*, follows that of *Judas* in the Book of Maccabees; and the one after, *Joshua*, is similar to *Judas* in its story. Both went down well when they were given in the 1748 season. Morell tells an amusing tale about his collaboration with Handel:

'The next year he desired another [libretto] and I gave him *Alexander Balus* . . . as to the last Air, . . . when Mr. Handell first read it, he cried out "D—n your Iambics". "Don't put yourself in a passion, they are easily Trochees".[1] "Trochees, what are Trochees?" "Why, the very reverse of Iambics, by leaving out a syllable in every line, as instead of

u — | u —| u   —| u   —
Convey me to some peaceful shore,

—   u| — u | —   u   —
Lead me to some peaceful shore."

"That is what I want. I will step into the parlour, and alter them immediately." I went down and returned with them altered in about 3 minutes; when he would have them as they were [*i.e.* in Morell's original form], and set them most delightfully accompanied with only a quaver, and a rest of 3 quavers.'

Summer 1748 saw the composition of another two oratorios, which could hardly be more different: *Solomon*, on a grand, pageant-like scale, with elaborate and rich-sounding choruses; and *Susanna*, almost in the style of a light opera. These were given in 1749.

The peace of Aix-la-Chapelle had been signed in 1748 and, although the war that ended did not directly involve Britain, celebrations were planned in London. Among them was a firework display in Green Park. Handel was

[1] Iambics are lines based on the rhythm u– (short-long); trochees are –u (long-short).

Figure 18. 'A View of the Magnificent Structure erected for the Fire Works'

asked to write music for the occasion. At first the king, who supervised all the arrangements, objected to having music; then he changed his mind, when told that only 'martial instruments' would be used (wind instruments and drums). But Handel, after he had started work on the music, decided that he couldn't manage without strings. Almost certainly Handel got his own way.

Then it was decided to have a rehearsal of the music, open to the public, in Vauxhall Gardens. Handel again objected, but this time he was overruled. The rehearsal duly took place, and the reports said that 12,000 people were present—causing a three-hour traffic jam on London Bridge. When it came to the performance, part of the structure built for the fireworks caught fire. And it rained. But the music was a success. Opposite is an excerpt from it, called 'La Réjouissance' ('The Rejoicing').

Handel gave a second performance of his *Music for the Royal Fireworks* a few weeks later. In London there was a hospital for foundlings, dependent on charity for its upkeep. We saw how Handel willingly gave to the Dublin charitable institutions. In London too he was ready to do so, and he offered to give a concert in aid of the hospital in May 1749. Members of the royal family and other influential people came; they heard the *Fireworks Music*, a new anthem, part of *Solomon*, and other pieces. The next year Handel was elected a Governor of the hospital, and he started a series of annual charity performances there of *Messiah* (using about twenty-five singers and an orchestra of thirty-five). The Foundling Hospital still owns an original copy of the *Messiah* manuscript.

By this time Handel was sixty-five years old; not a bad age for a man to reach in the eighteenth century. His health was good, although he was very fat indeed. He had always enjoyed eating, but even by the generous eighteenth-century standards of gluttony he was remarkable. Burney wrote: 'Nature required a great sustenance . . . to support so huge a mass'—though perhaps the mass wouldn't have been so huge if the sustenance had been less great!

An artist of the time, Joseph Goupy, commented on Handel's greed in a caricature. (Handel was a lover of art—he owned some Rembrandt pictures and had friends among artists.) Once, the story goes, Goupy was Handel's guest at a meal; Handel excused himself for a moment, and through a half-open door Goupy saw him swigging a bottle of choice wine. The caricature (see p. 59) was a cruel repayment even of this inhospitable act.

But Handel was not a mean man. He had a wide circle of friends, in many classes of society. He treated his patrons with the extreme civility normal

Music for the Royal Fireworks: 'La Réjouissance'

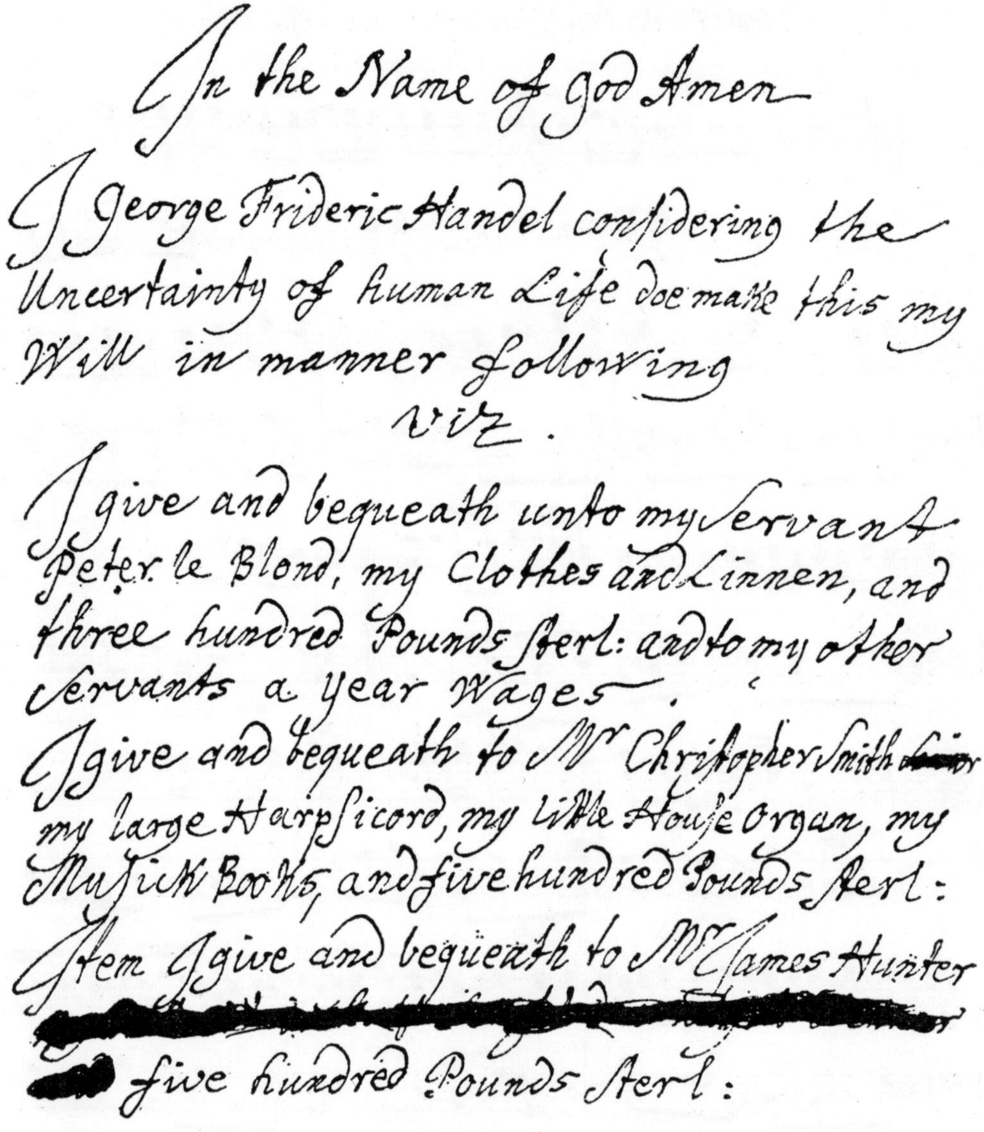

In the Name of god Amen

I George Frideric Handel considering the Uncertainty of human Life doe make this my Will in manner following
viz .

I give and bequeath unto my Servant Peter le Blond, my Clothes and Linnen, and three hundred Pounds sterl: and to my other Servants a year Wages .

I give and bequeath to Mr Christopher Smith my large Harpsicord, my little House Organ, my Musick Books, and five hundred Pounds sterl :

Item I give and bequeath to Mr James Hunter ~~five hundred Pounds sterl~~ five hundred Pounds sterl :

Figure 19 (*above aud opposite*). Handel's will (to which he later added four codicils giving legacies to his friends)

in those days. Often he was invited to stay with his wealthy friends and patrons at their country homes. He must have been acquainted with people in the literary world—Gay, Pope, and Smollett probably came into contact with him—and we know from the legacies in his will that he had friends in the professional and business worlds. And his oldest friends, J. C. Schmidt

84

I give and bequeath to my Cousin Christian Gottlieb Handel
of Coppenhagen one hundred Pounds Sterl:

Item I give and bequeath to my Cousin Magister Christian
August Roth of Halle in Saxony one hundred Pounds Sterl:

Item I give and bequeath to my Cousin the Widow of
George Taust, Pastor of Giebichenstein near Halle in
Saxony three hundred Pounds Sterl.
and to Her six Children each two hundred Pounds Sterl:
All the next and residue of my Estate in Bank Annuity's.
~~South Sea~~
~~Annuity's~~ or of what soever Kind or Nature,
I give and bequeath unto my Dear Niece
Johanna Friderica Floerken of Gotha in Saxony
(born Michäelsen in Halle) whom I make my
Sole Exec[trix] of this my last Will
- In wittness Whereof I have hereunto set my hand
this 1 Day of June 1750

George Frideric Handel

and his musically gifted son, were always close, except during a period of estrangement after a bitter quarrel.

One unfailing friend and supporter, from the time he first arrived in England, was the little girl whom we met on p. 22, Mary Granville. Apart from some years in Dublin, with her second husband, she lived mainly in

London, and was a constant attender at his concerts. Handel often visited her for musical evenings. This is how she described one of them, in 1734, in a letter to a friend:

'I must tell you of a little entertainment of music I had last week . . . I had Lady Rich and her daughter, Lady Cath. Hanmer and her husband, Mr. and Mrs. Percival, Sir John Stanley and my brother, Mrs. Donellan, Strada and Mr. Coot. Lord Shaftesbury begged of Mr. Percival to bring him, and being a *profess'd friend* of Mr. Handel (who was here also) *was admitted;* I never was so *well* entertained at *an opera*! Mr. Handel was in the best humour in the world, and played lessons and accompanied Strada and all the ladies that sang from seven o' the clock till eleven. I gave them tea and coffee, and about half an hour after nine had a salver brought in of chocolate, mulled white wine and biscuits. Everybody was easy and seemed pleased . . .'

Although ageing and troubled by weak eyesight, Handel continued his oratorio seasons during these last years of his life. The 1750 season saw one new work performed—*Theodora*, his only English oratorio (*Messiah* apart) on a Christian subject, and one of the few with a wholly tragic ending. The public did not much like it. One friend expressed sympathy over the poor attendances; Handel replied that the music sounded better in an empty theatre. Another friend asked for some free tickets for a *Messiah* performance; to this one Handel replied (in Burney's idea of his accent): 'Oh your sarvant, mein Herren! you are tamnaple tainty! you would not go to *Teodora*—der was room enough to tance dere, when dat was perform.'

In the summer of 1750 Handel paid his last visit to Germany, probably to see old friends and his relatives in Halle. He was badly hurt when his coach overturned, but, back in London by the end of the year, he started work on a new oratorio, *Jephtha*. During February he had to put work aside because of his failing eyesight; this happened while he was working on a chorus, 'How dark, O Lord, are thy decrees, All hid from mortal sight'. After taking the waters at Bath and Cheltenham, his eyesight was no better. He consulted a surgeon, who was pessimistic, and suggested that Handel should go into partnership with the English composer and organist, John Stanley, who had been blind since infancy. To this Handel replied: 'Have you never read the Scriptures? Do you not remember? If the blind lead the blind, they both fall into the ditch.' Even now his humour did not desert him.

During the summer of 1751 he was able to complete *Jephtha*, which had its first performance the next season. This oratorio is about a leader of the

Figure 20. A page from the manuscript of *Jephtha*; in the bottom right-hand corner is Handel's note about breaking off composition because of his failing sight
(*see opposite page*)

army who promises to sacrifice to God the first creature he meets on his victorious return; in fact, it is his own daughter who comes to meet him, and, although everyone tries to persuade him not to carry out his vow, he resolves to do so. Finally she is spared by an angel's intervention. The story gives good opportunities for portraying character, especially of Jephtha himself and his daughter Iphis; though the main feeling behind it is that mere human beings have to accept the will of God. To the ageing Handel, now going blind, this must have seemed very real.

About this time he had to give up playing organ concertos at the oratorio performances. At first he was able to play them from memory, but later he had to make up the solo part as he went along, indicating to the orchestra when they should come in. He had always relied to some extent on improvisation, as the concertos left in manuscript at his death (and then published, as his Op. 7) show. There are gaps in the music, with simply 'Org. ad libitum' written above them. Burney tells how his audiences were affected by seeing him, sightless:

'To see him led to the organ and then conducted towards the audience to make his accustomed obeisance, was a sight so truly afflicting and deplorable to persons of sensibility, as greatly diminished their pleasure in hearing him perform.'

And an old patron, the Countess of Shaftesbury, described one performance as 'a melancholy pleasure, as drew tears of sorrow to see the great though unhappy Handel, dejected, wan, and dark, sitting by, not playing on the harpsichord, and to think how his light had been spent by *being overplied in music's cause*'. On that occasion the audience were so unkind as not even to applaud; but on another, during the song 'Total Eclipse' (*Samson*; see pp. 71–3), many were in tears.

Generally, however, the oratorio seasons, now given during Lent, grew steadily in popularity. There were no more new compositions now, though in 1757 Handel revised a work written long before, *The Triumph of Time and Truth*. Presumably he dictated what he wanted to J. C. Smith (Schmidt's son, now his secretary).

In 1758, Handel went to Tunbridge Wells, where a famous oculist operated on him (the same man had operated, unsuccessfully, on Bach). At first there was hope, but soon darkness descended again. The 1759 oratorio season was given as usual, ending with three performances of *Messiah*, the last on April 6. After that performance Handel had intended to go to Bath, but was so ill that he had to be taken home to bed.

We can leave the rest of the story to a friend of Handel's, the Bond Street perfumer James Smyth, who wrote a letter to another close friend, Mary Granville's brother Bernard.

'According to your request to me when you left London, that I would let you know when our good friend departed this life, on Saturday last [April 14] at 8 o'clock in the morn died the great and good Mr. Handel. He was sensible to the last moment; made a codicil to his will on Tuesday, ordered to be buried privately in Westminster Abbey, and a monument not to exceed £600 for him. I had the pleasure to reconcile him to his old friends; he saw them and forgave them, and let all their legacies stand! In the codicil he left many legacies to his friends, and among the rest he left me £500, and has left to you the two pictures *you formerly gave him*. He took leave of all his friends on Friday morning, and desired to see nobody but the Doctor and Apothecary and myself. At 7 o'clock in the evening he took leave of me, and told me we "should meet again"; as soon as I was gone he told his servant "*not* to let me come to him any more, for that he had *now done with the world*". He died as he lived—a good *Christian*, with a true sense of his duty to God and man, and in perfect charity with all the world . . .'

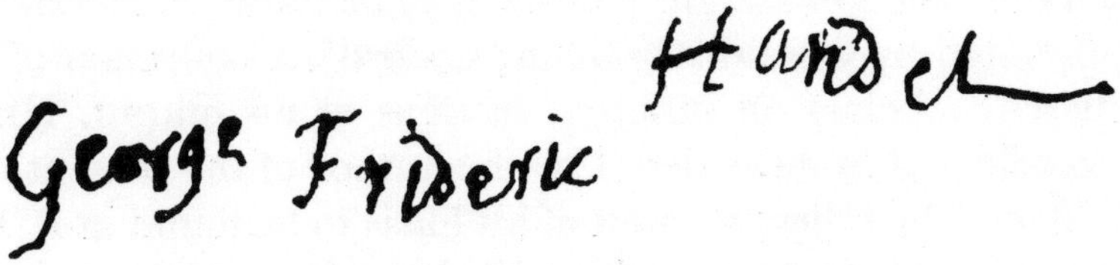

Figure 21. Handel's signature, from a codicil to his will

Suggestions for Further Reading

A useful discussion of Handel's music is to be found in *Handel: A Symposium* (edited by Gerald Abraham; Oxford), a collection of essays by different scholars on different sections of his output. His life and music are considered in more detail by the author of the present volume in *Handel* (Calder). The fullest account of his life is to be found in P. H. Lang's *Handel* (Faber, London; Norton, New York), a large-scale study in which the general intellectual climate in which Handel worked is considered in great detail. Winton Dean's *Handel's Dramatic Oratorios and Masques* (Oxford) is a searching and very rewarding study of his oratorios, in particular of his dramatic style in them; the same author has written a smaller book on his methods in the operas. Anyone particularly interested in *Messiah* will find fascination in the detective work on its history contained in Watkins Shaw's *A Companion to Handel's 'Messiah'* (Novello). Finally, O. E. Deutsch's *Handel: A Documentary Biography* (Black, London; Norton, New York) is a collection of basic biographical material; in it all the known contemporary references to Handel (letters, advertisements, accounts and the like) are printed in full.

Outline List of Handel's Works

Vocal

    42 operas (some incomplete, some not surviving)

    19 oratorios

    10 secular choral works

    105 Italian cantatas

    25 Italian duets and trios

    A few cantatas and songs in English, Italian, German, French, and Spanish

    Sacred works, including 11 Chandos anthems, three Te Deum settings, funeral and wedding anthems, 4 coronation anthems, 9 Latin works, German sacred songs

Orchestral

    12 Grand Concertos, Op. 6

    6 concertos, Op. 3, for strings and wind

    6 organ concertos, Op. 4

    6 organ concertos, Op. 7

    9 miscellaneous organ concertos (partly arrangements)

    Water Music

    Music for the Royal Fireworks

    3 oboe concertos

    3 concertos for double wind band and strings

    Other miscellaneous concertos

Chamber and instrumental works

    Sonatas for solo instrument (violin, flute, recorder, oboe) and continuo: about 20, including 14, Op. 1

    Trio sonatas for 2 instruments (violins, flutes, oboes) and continuo: about 22, including 6, Op. 2, and 7, Op. 5

    Overture for 2 clarinets and horn

    2 books each of 8 suites for harpsichord; 2 books of fugues

    Many miscellaneous keyboard pieces

Index

Page numbers in *italics* denote illustrations or music examples.

Index

Index